The
Way to

ETERNAL
LIFE

Contemporary Reflections on the
Traditional Stations of the Cross

By Br. Francis de Sales Wagner, O.S.B.

~
Illustrations by Fr. Donald Walpole, O.S.B.

Path of Life Publications
Spiritual Food for the Christian Journey from **Abbey Press**

Stations of the Cross artwork by Fr. Donald Walpole, O.S.B.,
photograph of Fr. Donald,
and *Christus* image by Dom Gregory de Wit, O.S.B.,
courtesy of Saint Meinrad Archabbey

Photographs of Stations by Mary E. Bolin
Cover and book design by Mary E. Bolin

Scripture quotations from New Revised Standard Version

ISBN 978-0-87029-519-5
Library of Congress 2012953408

Published by Abbey Press
1 Hill Drive • St. Meinrad, IN 47577
Printed by Abbey Press in United States of America
www.pathoflifebooks.com

Fr. Donald Walpole, O.S.B.
May 1, 1917 — January 27, 2012

Requiescat in pace

He has borne our infirmities
and carried our diseases;
yet we accounted him stricken,
struck down by God, and afflicted.

But he was wounded for our transgressions,
crushed for our iniquities;
upon him was the punishment that made us whole,
and by his bruises we are healed.

Isaiah 53:4-5

Introduction

"If any want to become my followers,
let them deny themselves
and take up their cross daily
and follow me."

Luke 9:23

A young man whose wisdom belied his age once said to me: "Don't worry about being original. Just be true." That is sound advice for anyone entrusted with spreading the Good News of Jesus Christ—which includes all baptized Christians. We need not—indeed, *dare* not—invent anything or pretend to be someone we're not. We simply must speak the truth—*be* the truth. And what is truth as far as Christians are concerned? Allow me to reply by stringing together (*not inventing!*) a few key passages of Scripture:

> God so loved the world that he gave his only Son, so that everyone who believes in him may not perish but may have eternal life. God did not send the Son into the world to

condemn the world, but in order that the world might be saved through him. If any wish to become his followers, let them deny themselves and take up their cross daily and follow him. For if we have been united with him in a death like his, we will certainly be united with him in a resurrection like his. Go therefore, and make disciples of all nations, baptizing them in the name of the Father and of the Son and of the Holy Spirit, and teaching them to obey everything that he commanded. Remember, he is with you always, to the end of the age. Jesus Christ is the same yesterday and today and forever" (cf. John 3:16-17; Luke 9:23; Romans 6:5; Matthew 28:19-20; Hebrews 13:8).

This compendium of the Gospel, so to speak, contains some hard certainties upon which we are likely to stub our toes occasionally. It speaks of the unbounded mercy of God, of redemption, and of eternal life (not like *this* life, but with a "resurrection like his"). It speaks of the ubiquitous and unchanging qualities of God. Those are good; we like all that. However, it also speaks of self-denial, toil, and obedience. Moreover, it offers no escape clause from what we fear most—suffering and death. It presents us with the cross. We don't like all that quite as much. *How can God permit it?*

Of course, I cannot offer an original response to that question, and this book will not attempt to do so. All anyone can do is retell or rearticulate the truth, because it's already been said or written; it already *is*. And yet the question continues to linger. No matter how hard we try, we can neither answer nor dismiss it. It not only refuses to go away, but somehow manages to impel us to keep poking and prodding in search of a clue—any clue. Such is the

power of truth. We know it's there; we can try to deny or ig-
nore it; we can try to explain it away or offer alternatives.
We can try to denounce it outright. And yet, it has an un-
speakable hold on us. Resistance is futile, it seems. If there is
no truth in the question, then why do we persist in asking it,
like Pontius Pilate examining Jesus: "What is truth?" (John
18:38) We want answers, of course, but the truth is that
they're all around us, woven into the fabric of our lives.
That is a pretty important clue in itself.

For instance, in our sports-obsessed culture (in the
spirit of truth, I must disclose that I am an avid baseball
fan), we value offensive linemen in football who sacrifice
their bodies in a mass of flying flesh to clear the way for a
running back toting a ball. If he scores a touchdown, everyone notices him, not the linemen. In baseball, we cheer a
batter who sacrifices himself as a potential hitter and base
runner by laying down a perfect bunt that advances others
on the base paths. The latter will move on to potential scor-
ing position. The batter, however, is out (usually). Hence the
term: "take one for the team." The self is surrendered in
pursuit of a greater good for many. On a more individual
athletic level, a marathon runner maintains a punishing
training regimen in preparation for an upcoming race. She
gives up personal comfort, desires, and other pursuits to
focus on winning a contest that may be months away—and
which only one person out of perhaps thousands will prove
victorious. Her eyes are fixed solely on the prize.

Of course, there are more worthwhile analogies from
the non-sports world of daily life: a firefighter who endan-
gers self to rescue another's being or property; a family

bread-winner who works more than one job to help make ends meet; anyone who, in various ways, escapes notice and quite possibly endures personal deprivation or disgrace while quietly contributing in some life-giving way to another's welfare.

The value underlying such actions is something we recognize as being good, even if we are not particularly adept at practicing it ourselves. While it may be argued that "taking one for the team" or delaying gratification to keep one's eyes on a greater prize is becoming less common in today's world, we admire it when we see it, and are perhaps inspired to do likewise. It seems to be a truth at the core of our being no matter how strenuously our nature objects— like the will that struggles to rouse us from sleep to confront the day and its challenges when all we truly desire is to burrow back underneath the bedcovers. Our nature resists, but grace needs to discover the truth, to tell the truth, to *be* the truth. It wants to involve us in the story that is our lives— in humanity's story.

"Everyone who belongs to the truth listens to my voice," Jesus told Pontius Pilate. "I am the way, and the truth, and the life." (John 18:37; 14:6). That grace rousing us from sleep, so to speak, is the voice of Christ from the cross. *How can God permit it?* Because he loves us too much not to permit it. While this is hardly the place for a theological discourse on free will and the effects of original sin, the Cross offers us a way out—the *only* way out. And to be effective, it requires our cooperation—the loving gift of self in response to God's love for us. Remarkably, God desires to involve us in his merciful act of redemption.

At the risk of carrying the sports analogies above too far, the offensive linemen may block and the batter may bunt, but the running back and base runners must do their part. We are the runners for whom God makes the ultimate sacrifice (cf. Philippians 2:5-11), taking on our load, sacrificing himself, and clearing the way for us to race toward the prize of eternal life. While football and baseball were not around in St. Paul's day, he was nonetheless familiar with the principle: "Athletes exercise self-control in all things; they do it to receive a perishable garland, but we an imperishable one" (1 Corinthians 9:25).

While the notion of self-sacrifice for the good of others is acceptable (if not always observed), the cross is a scandal for many—even among Christians. It always has been. The disciples of Jesus struggled with the notion themselves. Their expectations were not met. They envisioned an all-powerful Messiah asserting political might in establishing an earthbound kingdom. Salvation was supposed to be about wealth and health and influence. Jesus stood all that on its head. He pointed to what prophets like Isaiah had foretold about a Suffering Servant, that the Christ would be pierced for human faults, crushed for our sins (cf. Isaiah 53:5). Blessed are the poor, he said, and those who mourn, the meek, the merciful (cf. Matthew 5:3-11). God came to save all by being the servant of all, and those who wish "to become my followers, let them deny themselves and take up their cross daily and follow me" (Luke 9:23).

This was incomprehensible and unacceptable. No matter how much he taught or how many miracles Jesus performed, the disciples didn't get it. It was only in view of his later Resurrection and the insight gained by the subsequent descent of the Holy Spirit that things began to come together. Then, those first Christians began to go out into the world to tell the truth, to be the truth, by proclaiming Christ crucified. By his wounds, we have been healed—an unimaginable but far superior outcome compared with what they first had in mind (cf. 1 Peter 2:24).

Centuries later, the Cross still disturbs us. Suffering and sin are realities we'd rather not think about. Do we also subscribe to a gospel of wealth, health, and influence? While it certainly isn't beneficial to focus solely on our sorrows, it's also harmful to push the Cross aside as if it doesn't exist. When we push the Cross aside, we push aside freely offered grace. The Cross, Jesus tells us repeatedly throughout the gospels, is the gateway to eternal life. Christ crucified gives meaning to what otherwise is pure madness, decay, and death. As the French poet Paul Claudel said, "Jesus did not come to remove suffering, or to explain it, but to fill it with his presence." He became part of our suffering, part of humanity's story, in order to redeem it from within, and thereby involving us in his divine work of redemption. "When I am lifted up from the earth, I will draw all people to myself," Jesus said (John 12:32).

Here we confront the importance of the Incarnation of Christ in our daily lives—today. The Cross of Christ is not something we merely recall occasionally or fear that we carry all alone. It is our story, too, and his story is ours. It's why "the Word became flesh and lived among us" (John 1:14). As his disciples, we are called to make Christ present in the world through Word, Sacrament, and the example of a holy life; first, however, we must discern how Christ is present and working in our own lives, and deep within our very souls. This is Good News intended to give us hope along the way to eternal life. And so (to borrow a few phrases from Dom Hubert van Zeller in *Approach to Calvary*), when we are tempted to push the Cross aside, to neglect the Christian reality of necessary atonement, to disconnect our suffering from the Fall and from the Redemption and Resurrection that reverses the curse of Adam, we must recall Jesus' words to us: "Blessed is anyone who takes no offense at me" (Luke 7:23).

Viewed through the eyes of faith, the Cross offers us not an escape from our troubles, but a means by which the unholy is sanctified and death is transformed into sure and certain life. "There are times," St. Jerome wrote, "when evils become the occasion of blessings and when God causes good results to follow from the sinful designs of men. A manifest example of this is the case of Joseph [Genesis 37, 45], whom his brothers, moved by jealousy, sold to the Ishmaelites for twenty pieces of silver. As things turned out, this crime against Joseph marked the beginning of all manner of benefits for the father and brothers of Joseph and for the whole land of Egypt, so that Joseph could later say to his brothers: 'Even though you meant harm to me, God meant it for good.'"

In my own life, I have slowly come to recognize that our crosses are not obstacles as much as they are opportunities for transformation and healing in ways that go beyond our present difficulties (though I make no claim of having capitalized on all those opportunities!). Pain, toil, sorrow, disease, and death are realities for each of us—part of the human experience. However, through the Cross, the Incarnation of Christ bridges the gap between humanity and divinity, between time and eternity. We don't merely attempt to imitate the life, death, and resurrection of Christ. We *are* the life, death, and resurrection of Christ. We are the Church—the Body of Christ—in the world, and through it, he not only suffers for us, but with us, and we with him. As St. Paul wrote: "If we have been united with him in a death like his, we will certainly be united with him in a resurrection like his" (Romans 6:5).

Living this mystery of faith through our trials leads to the startling yet comforting truth: We are not merely bystanders in God's saving plan, and not only benefactors. By the grace of God, through Christ, and with the aid of the Holy Spirit, we are *partners.* Working in tandem with Christ, we shoulder the yoke of the Cross for one another and for all others. Self-giving then clears the way for self-fulfillment in the resurrected Body of Christ. In the end, the paradox of the Cross reveals humanity's brightest hope within its darkest moment. God comes to us precisely where we don't look for him. Our weakness is turned into his strength. Our hurt is healed in unexpected ways. "Where sin increased, grace abounded all the more" (Romans 5:20).

This is the truth for all those baptized in Christ—"buried with him by baptism into death, so that, just as Christ was raised from the dead by the glory of the Father, so we too might walk in newness of life" (Romans 6:4). The newness of life for which we strive, as St. Paul said, is transformation by the renewal of our minds, so that we may discern the will of God (Romans 12:2). The way to Eternal Life is through the Cross. It's not original, but it's the truth.

The present volume is intended to be an extended meditation on that mystery. It is not a devotional guide on the Stations of the Cross in the traditional sense like many existing books and pamphlets—though it can certainly be used as such, if one has the time. Rather, each Station offers avenues of reflection connecting the Cross of Christ with our own. Most are the fruit of my own prayer and study (one exception being the Twelfth Station, where it seemed appropriate to allow some short passages from the Gospel of John to speak for themselves). The tone (hopefully) is both contemplative and pastoral, and the book is designed to be read slowly and pondered over time. Each reflection is followed by a prayer—either an original composition as a result of my own meditation, or an appropriate excerpt from the Psalms. All in all, the book is designed to be a meditative tool to draw the reader deeper into his or her own understanding of the mystery of the Cross.

Scripture citations are numerous throughout the reflections in an effort to emphasize the primary theme of the Word made Flesh—both in the life of Christ and in our own daily lives. I took this cue from the late Fr. Donald Walpole, O.S.B., whose rich accompanying artwork includes numerous Latin inscriptions—most of them from Scripture, and many from the Psalms. For this reason, it may be useful to keep a Bible handy while reading this book.

Beneath the artwork for each Station is the English translation of the Latin inscription, provided by my confreres Fr. Simeon Daly, O.S.B., a contemporary of Fr. Donald's who committed himself to cataloguing the artist's vast collection of work (see Fr. Donald's short biography at the end of the book) and Fr. Harry Hagan, O.S.B., a Scripture scholar. Fr. Simeon, who died at age 90 as this book neared publication, dedicated much of his monastic career to preserving many important works, serving as the Archabbey's librarian for nearly 50 years. Fr. Harry, who was instrumental in returning the Stations to prominent display after a long period in storage, says that the Stations are some of Fr. Donald's best work. While I have slightly adapted some of the inscription translations for the sake of brevity and ease of use for the purposes of this volume, I am indebted to Fr. Simeon and Fr. Harry not only for their assistance, but also their encouragement and example. Fr. Simeon's own reflections in booklets produced for alumni by the Saint Meinrad Archabbey Development Department were the inspirational seeds of the present publication.

As I have mentioned, *most* of Fr. Donald's inscriptions are taken directly from Scripture in relation to the action shown in each panel. However, since several are either from other sources (such as a line from a traditional hymn) or are given new contexts in relation to the scene of a particular Station, I have not included the direct citations. Instead, my hope is that the reader will accept the inscriptions at face value as a means of entering more fully into contemplating each Station. Generally speaking, I have written each reflection in view of the corresponding artwork (more closely for some than others), but it is worth mentioning that Fr. Donald's Stations of the Cross—which existed decades before this book—serve as a splendid meditation in and of themselves, and I hope the English translations are an aid in that respect.

For those who are interested in seeing the Stations in person, they now adorn the walls of the crypt chapel (St. Joseph Oratory) beneath the Archabbey Church of Our Lady of Einsiedeln at Saint Meinrad in southern Indiana—the monastery which Fr. Donald, Fr. Simeon, Fr. Harry, and myself, in turn, have called home. They were originally commissioned for the Archabbey Church, and were affixed to the church walls in the mid-1950s. They were removed during the church's renovation in 1968, and have been displayed in the crypt since 1996.

One point worth noting is the similarity in style between the work of Fr. Donald and that of Dom Gregory de Wit, whose large figure of the risen Christ adorns the apse of the Archabbey Church. This *Christus* image has been employed for the epilogue of this book. De Wit was a Belgian monk who spent time in the United States and at Saint Meinrad in the late 1930s and 1940s. As a young monk, Fr. Donald spent a great deal of time assisting him, and he acknowledged that de Wit was a tremendous influence on him artistically. The artwork of both Fr. Donald and de Wit are prominent throughout the campus of Saint Meinrad, and while the student had his own style, the master's influence on the student's work is noticeable.

The *Christus* image seemed fitting to include because it represents what the Stations of the Cross—our pilgrim journey on earth—ultimately move toward: Eternal Life in Christ. The large Greek letters above the figure of the risen Christ in the image stand for *Iesous Christos* (Jesus Christ), and in his left hand, Christ holds the book of life, inscribed with the Latin words *Ego Sum Vita*, or "I am the Life," which is an excerpt from John 14:6 ("I am the way, and the truth, and the life").

Fr. Donald's Stations of the Cross, meanwhile, are striking in their simplicity and in their poignancy. He employs the natural surface of the wood panels as his background, and white, black, and red as his primary colors—strokes of grace, as it were. The images and their very mode of presentation suggest the Incarnation of Christ in a profound way. Grace builds on nature, with the inscriptions—the Word of God—mediating between the two.

While I only knew Fr. Donald for the last five-and-a-half years of his life (he was 94 when he died), he seemed to truly personify both the approach to his artwork and the theme of the reflections in this book. He certainly had his crosses, physical limitations, and personal faults; but, he was the happiest 94-year-old I ever met. He was a faithful monk, loved a good joke, had a sharp memory and a penchant for telling stories, and he took absolutely no prisoners during card games.

As a novice, I had the opportunity to spend some time talking with Fr. Donald about his artwork and his past, and what struck me the most about the experience was that he vividly recalled the people involved with each of his projects, who provided assistance, and how each work came together, right down to the precise materials that were used. There was a genuine heartiness to the man, but also a depth that at first appeared to belie his joviality—but which I later realized was its source. He arose each morning at 4 a.m., sitting in the silence of the monastery calefactory to ponder the mysteries of God more than an hour before the bell for Vigils summoned the rest of us to prayer. Fr. Donald's feet were firmly planted on the ground, but his mind was set on things that are from above (cf. Colossians 3:2).

Similarly, we move forward on this earthly journey to eternal life, embracing the Cross with our eyes fixed on the prize to which God calls us upwards to receive in Christ (cf. Philippians 3:10-14). Impelled by love, we race for the finish, progressing (as the following Station reflections do) from the foot of the cross to its head, from the human to divine, from the surface to the depths, from the exterior to the interior, from the particular to the universal, from the momentary to the timeless. As we do, we may not have all the answers, but we can faithfully live the questions, believing this truth: The Cross will always be a sign of contradiction for some, but it is meant to be a sign of love for all.

> *"You spare all things, for they are yours,*
> *O Lord, you who love the living."*

Wisdom 11:26

Br. Francis de Sales Wagner, O.S.B.
Saint Meinrad Archabbey, September 14, 2012
Feast of the Exaltation of the Holy Cross

by THiS CROSS

Staggering under the weight,
strength is sapped.
Life is poured out,
anguish deeper than pain.

There is simply nothing left.

Nothing.

Welling up, this nothingness cries out.

Yet, its very sound is one of hope—faint but fearless:

"My God, my God, why have you forsaken me?"

Ears are opened to the voice
of sincerity, humility, faith.

I can hear my nothingness.

See my dignity.

Touch my identity.

Something sterner than death arises,
beating in harmony
with a force other than being.

There is light, and it sings.

This cross I have, I must need.
Why is beyond the mind's eye,
guarded by Truth and Love.

The reply rises softly, lingers, prods.

It is unmistakable.
Always present.
Rarely heard:

*"If any want to become my followers,
let them deny themselves
and take up their cross daily
and follow me."*

*"This is my Beloved Son,
with whom I am well pleased.
Listen to him."*

Yes! By his wounds, I have been healed.
Lord, help me with this cross.
Now I know it only makes sense
if it is borne for another's sake.

Mystery enlightens.

Weakness is made strong.

The back straightens; feet become steady.

This cross is still here.

But now it embraces all.

Through,
with,
in
One:
Truly,
this man
was the
Son of God.

My soul shall live for him,
declaring to all:
It is accomplished;
these things
the Lord
has done!
By this cross.

"*Let his blood be on us and on our children.*"
Volo*: "I am willing.*"
Fiat*: "Let it be.*"

god's designs

FIRST STATION
Jesus Is Condemned to Death

Life can often be unfair, and sometimes we may feel like we're all alone. Yet these challenging moments can also provide ripe opportunities for insight and growth. Even when we can't choose our circumstances, we can always choose how to react to them, what we may learn from them, and to believe that somewhere in the mix, God is present, redeeming the moment in a way we can't clearly recognize. As St. Paul says, "We know that all things work together for good for those who love God" (Romans 8:28).

As proof, Jesus stands before us an innocent yet condemned man. His very name means "God saves," and he himself tells us: "God did not send the Son into the world to condemn the world, but in order that the world might be saved through him. Those who believe are not condemned; but those who do not believe are condemned already, because they have not believed in the name of the only Son of God" (John 3:17-18). Paradoxically, to accomplish the work of redemption, Jesus willingly allows himself to be condemned to death on our behalf—the sinless for the sinful, the Second Adam for Adam, God for man. Pilate and those who cry out, "Crucify him!" are only instruments in a much deeper design of divine love.

God's love looks back at us through the face of Jesus, condemned to death so that we, his people, might have eternal life. His back is turned to Pilate, who sits in the shadows. Jesus, by contrast, stands in the light with an invitation for each one of us: "I am the light of the world. Whoever follows me will never walk in darkness but will have the light of life" (John 8:12).

PRAYER

Lord, you stood alone, an innocent man
sentenced to death, while I kneel before you,
sinful but granted eternal life
in the company of angels and saints.
Help me to recall this
when my life seems to get the best of me,
when it weighs me down,
and when I feel as though
no one is on my side.
On the other side of your trial,
abandonment, and death awaited the Resurrection.
Help me to grow in that light,
knowing you are always at my side,
and trusting that whatever happens,
you are at work, redeeming the moment.

"Behold, I come."
"My heart will not fear."

ACCEPTANCE

SECOND STATION
Jesus Receives the Cross

Each one of us meets the Cross at one point or another: A layoff notice; divorce; a car accident; cancer. Whether or not we experience life-altering circumstances such as these, we cannot escape much of life's more chronic trials: Strained relationships; the tedium of toil; uncertainty and dissatisfaction; loneliness; aging; grief over various losses, including that of loved ones; misunderstanding and insult; jealousy; anger; betrayal. Most difficult of all, perhaps, is living with imperfection—in ourselves, in those around us, and in the world.

Whatever its form, the Cross awaits us—not to punish or torture, but simply because ours is a broken world in need of redemption. Suffering itself is evil, and has its origins in humanity's turning toward evil rather than the good that God provides. However, suffering is not the end, and united with Jesus, it even becomes the means by which the wounds of the Body of Christ are ultimately healed (cf. Colossians 1:24; 1 Peter 2:24). For example, grief and loneliness can help open our eyes and ears to the needs of others in similar circumstances; the experience of being oppressed can make us strong defenders of the weak. And even if we are too weak to act, our prayers have unseen strength. If we are the Body of Christ—and we are!—then by sharing in his suffering, we also share in the transformation brought about by his Resurrection (cf. Romans 6:5).

Jesus looks heavenward, willingly accepting the cross he's received. On it, in his Body, is nailed all our suffering and sin. Jesus takes it all, and through his cross, the world is redeemed. Likewise, our crosses become openings for transformation, challenges to embrace, and opportunities for healing in ways that go beyond our present circumstances. It is fine to ask God to relieve suffering, and it is absolutely necessary to work toward alleviating suffering wherever we find it. Jesus did the same. However, we must also pray for the strength to patiently endure, and for the wisdom to be transformed by the spiritual insight that often comes to light only in the midst of trial.

PRAYER

Lord, for you all things are possible.
Remove this cross—
but only according to your will
(cf. Mark 14:36).
No matter what happens,
help me to patiently accept what I must bear;
give me the courage
to overcome what I am able;
and grant me the wisdom
to unite my suffering with that of Christ's,
so that I may become the person
you've called me to be.

CVRVATVS
SVM VSQVE
IN FINEM

"*I am bowed down to the very end.
I go mourning all the day long.*"

ASCENDING HUMILITY

THIRD STATION
Jesus Falls the First Time

When someone falls, our first instinct is to help them up. It awakens within us compassion that perhaps needed to be stirred a bit. If we look around us more intently, we'll see that many are falling in one way or another—whether physically, emotionally, or spiritually. Sometimes, it's easier to notice this from the ground—where we ourselves have fallen. Acknowledgement of our own humanity, our own fallen nature, strengthens our compassion for others.

It is here that the eyes of Christ meet ours. Jesus was fully human and fully divine. His human nature—

our nature—falls to the ground under the weight of the cross. On his shoulders, quite literally, rests the weight of the world, its people, and their sins. And it is heavy, so he stumbles.

But his divine nature—ours by grace—is able to get back up again and continue along the way of the cross. In him, with him, and through him, we also are lifted back up off the ground. Jesus' struggle, his compassion, and his self-sacrifice strengthen us to carry our cross, to overcome the burden of our own human nature. By this cross, we are lifted back to our feet, better equipped to recognize Christ in others and be Christ to them. With St. Paul, we can say: "I am now rejoicing in my sufferings for your sake, and in my flesh I am completing what is lacking in Christ's afflictions for the sake of his body, that is, the church" (Colossians 1:24).

PRAYER

I waited patiently for the Lord;
he inclined to me and heard my cry.

He drew me up from the desolate pit,
out of the miry bog,
and set my feet upon a rock,
making my steps secure.

Happy are those who make
the Lord their trust.

— Psalm 40

"*In your womb he has hidden himself.*"

A Mother's Eyes

FOURTH STATION
Jesus Meets His Blessed Mother

Who can withstand the gaze of a mother—whether it's a look of compassion, commendation, or consternation? Along the way of the cross, the path to eternal life, Mary comes face to face with the fruit of her womb. Jesus, the Son of God, was conceived by the Holy Spirit, but took on his human form through Mary, his mother—and therefore our mother. As the new Eve—the mother of all the living whose "yes" to God reverses the first Eve's "no" (cf. Genesis 3:6, 20; Luke 1:38; John 19:27)—she has a role to play in our redemption. As Simeon foretold when Mary and Joseph brought the infant Jesus to Jerusalem to present him to the Lord, "a soul will pierce your own soul, too" (Luke 2:35).

So it is that the same mother who bore, nurtured, and grieved Jesus does so for us. Gazing at her son, her hands clasped in prayer, she intercedes for each and every one of us—that the One borne of her womb will find life in all of us amid our own struggles and sorrows. And while she peered then into the face of her suffering son, she now gazes on us from the perspective of what is just beyond our burdened shoulders—Resurrection.

When our strength fails, let us always turn to Mary our Mother, who embraces in her arms the entire Body of Christ—whether as an infant wrapped in swaddling clothes or as an adult stripped of all dignity on the road to Calvary. With Mary's faithfulness, we are assured of grasping the mystery she pondered while on earth—that what is broken will emerge whole and transformed from an empty tomb at the dawn of eternal life.

PRAYER

*Mary, you fix your gaze eternally
on the mysteries of Jesus,
your son and our Lord, and in so doing,
you meet the entire Body of Christ along the way.
Ask him to help me do the same,
so that my every thought, word, and action
originates from, and is directed toward, Jesus,
whom I should love above all else.
As I bear my own cross in this life,
ask him to take hold of me,
to lift my body, heart, and soul to himself,
so that I may be strengthened,
and so that through me,
his love may radiate
to all souls in search of light.*

"*Who will stand with me?*"

Sharing the burden

FIFTH STATION
Simon of Cyrene Helps Jesus Carry His Cross

Simon is busy. He's already given his share. He's got plans, and they don't include getting involved in someone else's business. He's got his own problems. So, he tries to slip through the crowd, pretending not to notice. Suddenly, Providence touches his shoulder. Circumstances aren't asking—they're demanding.

Pressed into service, the soldiers lay the cross on him, and tell him to carry it behind Jesus. Fearful and reluctant, he pleads to be excused from such toil, such humiliation. "Why, me?" he asks.

Then his eyes meet those of Jesus, and their hearts speak as one: "Take my yoke upon you and learn from me; for I am gentle and humble in heart, and you will find rest for your souls. For my yoke is easy, and my burden is light" (Matthew 11:29-30).

The yoke is not used much in the modern world. It is a wooden harness used to guide oxen or other draft animals while plowing fields, a sight which would have been familiar in Jesus' time (and still is in some developing countries and within more traditional cultures). A yoke is a crossbar with two U-shaped pieces that encircle the necks of a pair of oxen, working in tandem. The load is shared equally. Used as a verb, "yoke" means to join or to unite.

The image is full of purpose and meaning. Working with each one of us under the yoke—or cross—is Christ. He works in tandem with us, encourages us, and promises joy beyond all knowing for those who "take my yoke upon you and learn from me." When we, like Simon, are pressed into service to bear a cross we didn't seek, we must pray for strength and recall that, in the end, the cross does not belong to us, but to Christ, who bears it for all. When we take up his yoke, we bear the load in tandem with him, and united with the entire Body of Christ.

PRAYER

Lord, we don't get to choose our crosses,
and it is difficult for us to see
and accept the reasons
they are thrust upon us.
Help me to take the yoke of Christ
upon my shoulders and learn from him.
This yoke—this cross—
only makes sense if it is not my own,
if it is borne for another's sake.
Somewhere, the Church is eternally strengthened
by my freely acknowledged weakness.
Help me then, to say yes,
to carry the cross for another and for all others,
so that I may find rest myself.

"Your face, O Lord, I shall seek."

THE FACE OF CHRIST

SIXTH STATION
Veronica Wipes the Face of Jesus

"Lord, you have made us for yourself," St. Augustine famously wrote in his *Confessions*. "Our heart is restless until it rests in you." Indeed, deep down—whether we know it or not—our souls yearn for God. Our deepest desire is for the God who made us, to see his face. It is God who knocks on the door of our hearts, and we remain restless until our hearts are opened and fixed on him alone. Much of Scripture, particularly the Psalms, expresses this desire: "My soul thirsts for God, for the living God. When shall I come and behold the face of God?" (Psalm 42:2).

On behalf of the ancient Israelites, Moses, prefiguring Christ, spoke to God "face to face, as one speaks to a friend" (Exodus 33:11). Jesus is our intermediary in this life. In him, we see God, as Jesus himself told us: "Whoever has seen me has seen the Father" (John 14:9). And if we follow Christ faithfully in this life while on the road to eternal life, we will see God's face in heaven (cf. Revelation 22:4).

However, as he was led to his crucifixion, Jesus' pained face was slapped, spat upon, and mocked. Perhaps even worse, it was ignored, as many passers-by turned their faces and pretended not to see. Others were too busy to notice. In our own way, we do the same more often than we realize, or care to acknowledge. Our passions—pride, greed, envy, lust, etc.— distort the face of God in our eyes, and tempt our gaze in the wrong direction. The desire to possess and control can easily overtake us, and before we know it, we've made ourselves "God."

The good news is that our merciful God never stops pursuing us in this life. He beckons us continually to turn away from our human tendencies and weaknesses, and to seek the face of Christ in our daily lives. No matter what we've done or failed to do, God is always ready to welcome us back (cf. Luke 15; Luke 23:39-43). So, we seek Christ in Scripture, in the Sacraments, in the life of the Church, in our crosses and daily circumstances, and in the faces of one another.

In this last respect, Veronica demonstrates for us an example of tremendous compassion through one small and simple act. Approaching Jesus, she steps through the surrounding cruelty and indifference, and with a cloth wipes the grime and exhaustion from his face. While she cannot lift the cross from his shoulders, her tenderness eases his burden, if only temporarily. Fixing her eyes on human weakness in the Body of Christ, she beholds the face of God, and her heart rests in him whose image she bears.

PRAYER

Lord, my restless heart longs to see your face.
Help me to see it more clearly
in the faces of all your children—
my brothers and sisters in Christ.
Assist me in reaching out
in love and compassion
to the physically or spiritually hungry,
the thirsty, the stranger,
the poor, the sick, and the imprisoned.
Grant me the courage
to resist the selfishness, indifference, and cruelty
of human nature,
and instead
minister to the weak, suffering, and needy—
for as Jesus said,
"Just as you did it to the least of my brothers,
you did it to me" (Matthew 25:40).

LVMBI MEI
IMPLETI
SVNT

ILLVSIO-
NIBVS

"My frame is filled with derision."

god Stoops

SEVENTH STATION
Jesus Falls the Second Time

Once again, Christ stumbles and falls to the ground. No matter how often we fail or feel like we simply lack the strength to continue along the way of life's troubles and trials, he is right there with us. Out of immense love for us, God lowers himself in Jesus to restore the dignity that sin has stripped from humanity. He shows us that the way to eternal life is one of self-sacrificing love and service. We are to give the love we receive through him.

The evening before his crucifixion, Jesus demonstrated this at the Last Supper through his own body language. John's Gospel (13:1-20) relates for us how Jesus, the Son of God, does something that even the lowliest slaves of the time did not do. He ties a towel around his waist, stoops in front of each of his disciples, and washes their feet. By doing this, Jesus alludes to the crucifixion that awaits him, but which cleanses and frees us—just as the slaughtered lamb at Passover saved the ancient Israelites in Egypt. "Do you know what I have done to you?" he asks. The question is just as pertinent for us today. "You also should do as I have done to you," he tells us.

Similarly, we recall this action each time we gather for the Eucharist, when we commemorate the Lord's Passion, Death, and Resurrection, and hear: "Jesus took bread, and after he had given thanks, broke it and said, 'This is my body that is for you. Do this in remembrance of me.'" Once again, God stoops to us, allows himself to be broken and shared among us, so that we who are so broken may together become the whole Christ, blessed and shared with all.

To stoop means to bend down, to lower oneself, to willingly become small in order to provide another dignity. Our Incarnate God debases himself in Jesus Christ, becoming an infant sleeping in a feeding trough, a man falling beneath the weight of the cross and crucified as a common criminal. And to strengthen us for the journey to eternal life, he becomes seemingly ordinary bread to be broken and eaten. His is the "punishment that made us whole" (Isaiah 53:5).

And so, like the woman caught in adultery (John 8:1-11), we who have fallen are raised up by Christ. We are restored to dignity by having our feet washed by the Master, who asks "Do you know what I have done to you?" The answer, once claimed, is the true source of joy, and provides the endurance we need not only to continue along the way of the cross, but to stoop and "wash the feet" of others. As St. Paul wrote: "The Father of mercies and the God of all consolation consoles us in all our affliction, so that we may be able to console those who are in any affliction with the consolation with which we ourselves are consoled by God" (2 Corinthians 1:3-4).

PRAYER

Lord, how often I stumble and fall,
but you are with me
every step of the way to lift me up,
to encourage and strengthen me.
Help me each day to truly realize
what you have done for me,
so that your mercy and grace
may inspire me to encourage
and strengthen others—
not from a position of superiority,
but from your own self-sacrificing love.

"Weep for yourselves and for your children."

Tears of Prayer

EIGHTH STATION
Jesus Meets the Women of Jerusalem

Unable to contain their sorrow and compassion for the suffering Jesus, a group of women following him along the way to Calvary openly mourns for him. "Daughters of Jerusalem," he tells them, "do not weep for me, but weep for yourselves and for your children" (Luke 23:28).

These words are not a rebuke but rather a divine commission. Jesus is asking them to set their sights on the eternal, to lament supernaturally the underlying reason for his necessary suffering—the evil that humanity habitually falls into, and the good it often neglects to do. He is encouraging them to realize that what he willingly does—bear our fallen human nature and undergo its just punishment—is a bountiful act of mercy which should give them untold joy and hope. In light of his Resurrection which will come three days later, all weeping and wailing over *him* will prove pointless. He is, after all, leading the way toward redemption and eternal life for all those willing to be his disciples.

Weep instead, Jesus says, for those among you who refuse to turn and follow me. In other words: *Pray for them*. Here, he asks his people—particularly the marginalized—to intercede not for him, but *with him,* on behalf of all humanity, imploring the Father's mercy, protection, and guidance. He entrusts to these women— and to us—the apostolate of prayer.

We all have a role to play in helping others along the way of the cross. We must "weep"—that is, intercede—for the entire Body of Christ, that through him we may all be brought to everlasting life. And, as Jesus says, we must do this while the "wood is green," while there is still time. When it is dry, it will be too late (cf. Luke 23:31).

PRAYER

May those who sow in tears
reap with shouts of joy.

Those who go out weeping,
bearing the seed for sowing,
shall come home with shouts of joy,
carrying their sheaves.

— Psalm 126

"They have made me an abomination to themselves."

PERFECTION IN WEAKNESS

NINTH STATION
Jesus Falls the Third Time

Weary and exhausted, Jesus collapses once again under the weight of humanity's pride. How often do we stop to consider how crushing the load was? Our own individual faults and failings are microscopic splinters within the massive beam of humanity's history which God himself carries on his shoulders. Yet, we all contribute to its weight. What love God must have for you—for us—to take on our weak humanity so that "where sin increased, grace abounded all the more" (Romans 5:20).

However, how often do we feel utterly overwhelmed by our weakness? We make sincere resolutions to change, but then fall once again. Typically, we do not stumble over new obstacles, but over the same old ones that continually trip us up no matter how hard we try to step around them. Frustration and despair can threaten to set in, and we are tempted to simply lie where we have fallen.

"Get up, let us be going," Jesus says at such moments (Matthew 26:46). Human failure in this life is to be expected. The point is to recognize it, acknowledge it, look to Christ for further strength and courage, and move on. As St. Francis de Sales wrote in his *Introduction to the Devout Life*: "We must not be disturbed at our imperfections, since for us perfection consists in fighting against them. We are always victorious provided that we are willing to fight." When we are weak—and admit it—it is then that we are strong (2 Corinthians 12:10). Perfection is not obtainable in this life. It is faithfulness that we pursue.

So, when we fall the third, fourth, or fiftieth time, let us look just as often over into the eyes of Jesus, who is with us each step of the way. With him, calling on the Father for strength, we are able to brace ourselves, slowly rise, and once again pick up our cross on the way to eternal life. Here, "love and faithfulness embrace" (cf. Psalm 85:10).

PRAYER

Lord, forgive me.
My pride is my shame,
but your mercy is my peace.
Strengthen me as I shoulder my cross,
and lift me up when I fall.
Help me to forgive myself and move on.
By your grace,
may I always extend to others
the mercy you've granted me,
so that one by one,
little by little, step by step,
we may all keep to your way.
You are our strength and salvation.

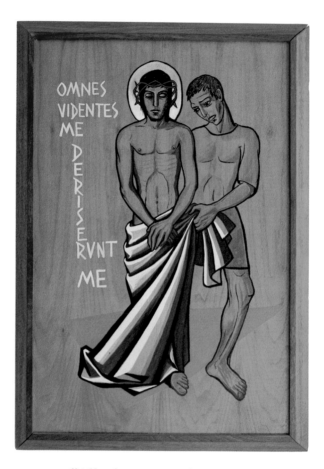

OMNES VIDENTES ME DERISERVNT ME

"All who see me deride me."

LETTING GO

TENTH STATION
Jesus Is Stripped of His Garments

"blessed are the poor in spirit," Jesus said in his Sermon on the Mount (Matthew 5:3). Before being nailed to the cross, Jesus is stripped of his garments in front of everyone. For our sake, he not only lets go of his human life, but his very dignity as a person. He is absolutely vulnerable, and that's not a position anyone enjoys.

Little by little, from birth to death, we must inevitably learn to let go of what we possess. A toddler is taught that not every toy belongs to him, that he must share with others. A grade-schooler must let go of the comfort and security provided by home and loved ones to experience the unknown in a wider circle of strange acquaintances. Newly married couples sacrifice their own desires and plans for the good of the family. Sickness and aging strip away our well-established habits which demonstrate self-reliance and independence.

Such lessons of diminishment—and many more like them—are common to us all. However, for the Christian on the way to eternal life, an additional underlying perspective is necessary, calling to mind the words of Jesus: "Those who want to save their life will lose it, and those who lose their life for my sake will save it" (Luke 9:24). We need to have an interior disposition of holy detachment. Figuratively speaking, if necessary, we must be willing to be stripped of all that clothes us, right down to our very dignity and absolute vulnerability.

Certainly, giving up something we'd like to keep is not easy for anyone, and a disposition of detachment usually takes a lifetime to understand, if not fully master. It's one of the most difficult demands of discipleship, but it lies at the heart of Christian living. Most of us will not be required to give up our lives as Jesus did, or as have many Christian martyrs. In addition, detachment is not simply about giving up money or material possessions. Detachment, rather, is about denying inordinate desires that would lead us astray from the path of life God holds out for us. As St. Paul wrote: "Those who *want to be rich* fall into temptation and are trapped by many senseless and harmful desires that plunge people into ruin and destruction. For the *love of money* is a root of all kinds of evil, and in their *eagerness to be rich* some have wandered away from the faith and pierced themselves with many pains. As for you, shun all this; pursue righteousness, godliness, faith, love, endurance, gentleness. Take hold of the eternal life to which you were called" (1 Timothy 6:9-12; *emphasis added*).

Notice that St. Paul does not say that the rich or those who have money fall into temptation. Rather, he speaks of those with *eagerness* to be rich, who are inordinately attached to their *love* of money—not money itself. Here, he speaks of holy detachment; he encourages us to be stripped of desires that, ironically, possess us and threaten to lead us away from the love of God—whether it involves money or any number of things.

With an honest interior examination, we can all compose lists of desires that need to be stripped away from our lives. We can give up some of our closely guarded time to someone who could really use it. We can give up an ancient grudge against someone. We can let go of our expectations about how something or someone should be and accept what is. We can allow the spotlight of recognition to be shifted from ourselves to someone else—who is, perhaps, even less deserving. We can let go of the need to be right, or the urge to respond to another's discourtesy with harsh words. We can refrain from disguising our envy with humorous put-downs and deal honestly with it instead. And we can allow our limitations—whether physical, emotional, or spiritual—to be opportunities for someone else to display charity, rather than stubbornly holding on to pride and refusing assistance.

All these are forms of giving up, of allowing ourselves to be stripped of our garments of attachments—and it hurts. It takes the love of Christ to hand such things over. In a sense, they are small deaths—but they lead to the inestimable treasure of everlasting life.

PRAYER

Lord, naked I came from my mother's womb,
and naked I shall return (cf. Job 1:21).
Grant me the grace to recognize
and embrace my absolute dependence
on your divine providence.
Be patient with me
as I learn to detach myself from any love
which does not have you
as its origin and end,
and help me to likewise bear with those
who also are in the process of being stripped
of what they hold dear.
Grant us all the eternal vision to realize
that as we let go of the desires that clothe us,
you stand ready to wrap us
in the garment of salvation
and the robe of righteousness
(cf. Isaiah 61:10; Luke 15:22).

DISPERSA SVNT
OMNIA OSSA
MEA

"Disjointed are all my bones."

Mercy

ELEVENTH STATION
Jesus Is Crucified

Here, perhaps more than anywhere else, we see God's undeniable mercy and undying love for each and every one of us. Humanity is incapable of redeeming our broken world, our wounded souls. The only possible solution is for God himself to step in as the Second Person of the Holy Trinity. His mercy pays our reparation—down to the last penny. By his wounds, we are healed.

Though he is innocent, Jesus willingly stretches out his body upon a cross reserved for the worst of criminals and insurrectionists. He does not struggle with or curse his tormentors, and he is unafraid. Being human, however, he certainly experiences the excruciating pain of having nails driven through limbs of his already scourged flesh—of being lifted high off the ground, fastened to the cross to slowly die of blood loss and asphyxiation. He suffers humiliation as the leaders and soldiers taunt him and scoff at him. Certainly, he feels sorrow for the injustice, the ignorance, and the indifference of God's people that led him to Calvary. And, as we all do at times, he feels abandoned, calling out in the opening words of Psalm 22: "My God, my God, why have you forsaken me?" (Mark 15:34).

However, there is no loss of hope, and no anger or vow of vengeance. Instead, remarkably, we hear this uttered from his lips:

"Father, forgive them; for they do not know what they are doing" (Luke 23:34).

That Scripture passage alone is worth meditating on for a lifetime. The innocent Son of God, being brutally killed, forgives his executioners—which includes each and every one of us. "God proves his love for us in that while we still were sinners, Christ died for us," because "God did not send the Son into the world to condemn the world, but in order that the world might be saved through him (Romans 5:8; John 3:17).

On that cross, in the Body of Christ, hangs our every fault, fear, and tear. Every ounce of it is put to death with him and transformed by the Resurrection three days later. God does what only God can: He makes the imperfect perfect, brings new life from death, changes mourning into dancing. "Death is swallowed up in victory" (1 Corinthians 15:54). This is not something we must earn. It is freely given to us. All we must do is open our hearts to accept it, and then, from gratitude, live this gift on the way to eternal life.

This is aptly demonstrated by the following passage from the Gospel of Luke:

> One of the criminals who were hanged there [on either side of Jesus] kept deriding him and saying, "Are you not the Messiah? Save yourself and us!" But the other rebuked him, saying, "Do you not fear God, since you are under the same sentence of condemnation? And we indeed have been condemned justly, for we are getting what we deserve for our deeds, but this man has done nothing wrong." Then he said, "Jesus, remember me when you come into your kingdom." He replied, "Truly, I tell you, today you will be with me in Paradise" (Luke 23:39-43).

This criminal's life had led him to share the fate of crucifixion. Yet at this crucial moment (his last chance!), he acknowledges his responsibility and recognizes Jesus for who he is. All he asks is that Jesus "remember" him. In response, Jesus promises much more than the criminal could ask for or imagine: "*Today*, you will be *with me* in *Paradise*." He asks for a small coin and instead receives the treasure of the Kingdom of Heaven!

Truly, God is compassion and love, rich in mercy. Let us be merciful, just as he is merciful (cf. Psalm 103:8; Luke 6:36).

PRAYER

If you, O Lord, should mark iniquities,
Lord, who could stand?
But there is forgiveness with you,
so that you may be revered.

For with the Lord there is steadfast love,
and with him is great power to redeem.

— Psalm 130

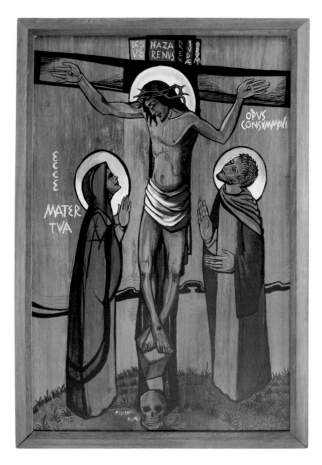

"I have finished the work."
Ecce Mater tua: *"Behold your mother."*

Lifted Up

TWELFTH STATION
Jesus Dies on the Cross

*Unless a grain of wheat
falls into the earth
and dies, it remains
just a single grain;
but if it dies,
it bears much fruit.*

*When I am lifted up
from the earth,
I will draw all people
to myself.*

It is finished.

John 12:24, 32; 19:30

PRAYER

My Lord and my God!
(cf. John 20:28)

"See if there is sorrow like my sorrow."

A MOTHER'S EMBRACE

THIRTEENTH STATION
Jesus Is Taken Down from the Cross

Look deeply into Mary's eyes as she cradles the body of her son Jesus after he has breathed his last. Can you follow her heart as she recalls her life with him, all that has led to this moment of sorrow? Are you able to discern how she pieces together the mysteries of Christ which she has pondered in her heart from the very beginning? (Luke 2:19). Is there a glint of hope behind the tears?

Mary knew from the moment the angel Gabriel appeared to her more than three decades earlier that she would bear the Son of God, but Gabriel did not explain how the lives of Jesus, Mary, and Joseph—the lives of *all* families—would play out. In faith, she simply had to live and put it all together as it happened, just as we do. Now, sitting beneath the cross used to crucify her son, is everything clear to her? Perhaps not; and yet…

Her thoughts travel back to that day many years ago when the three of them traveled to Jerusalem for Passover—the feast recalling their ancestors' miraculous escape from slavery in Egypt after eating a sacrificial meal of lamb, with the animal's blood marking their doorposts for safety (Exodus 12). After celebrating the feast in Jerusalem, Jesus became separated from Mary and Joseph. He remained behind, conversing with the temple elders, while they departed for home with their kinfolk, assuming the 12-year-old boy was somewhere in the crowd. Later realizing he was not among them, they grew frantic, and returned to Jerusalem. After three days, they found and embraced him in the temple, both relieved and upset, as any parents would be. And the boy said to them: "Why were you searching for me? Did you not know that I must be in my Father's house?" And they could not understand what he meant. (Luke 2:41-50). But now…

… The celebration of Passover—freedom gained through the blood of a lamb…Separation from Jesus…Discovery three days later…

Now, beneath the cross, her son's body in her arms, the words of the boy Jesus resound once again in Mary's heart, applicable to this moment: "Why are you searching for me? Do you not know that I must be in my Father's house?" Hints of promise begin opening up: Could it be that the boy being lost prefigured his death? Is it possible his discovery three days later in the temple now could mean…? Surely, Mary could not foresee the joy of Jesus' Resurrection three days later, but she gets a glimpse of the light to come, and so do we. Even in her grief and confusion, she is consoled and reassured. And so are we, since she is *our* mother, too. As Jesus said to his beloved disciple from the cross: "Here is your mother" (John 19:27).

PRAYER

Mary, Mother of the Church,
you are the hope of all Christian pilgrims
on the way to the heavenly Jerusalem,
where you and your son Jesus,
the Lamb of God, await us all.
Intercede for me,
so that I may grow in faith during my journey.
As I ponder the mysteries of Christ,
embrace me beneath the cross.
Comfort us all in our sorrow and distress,
and through the love of God,
help us to find Christ—
both in the temple of our hearts
and in the life to come.
The entire Body of Christ—wounded as it is—
is entrusted to your arms.
Pray for us.

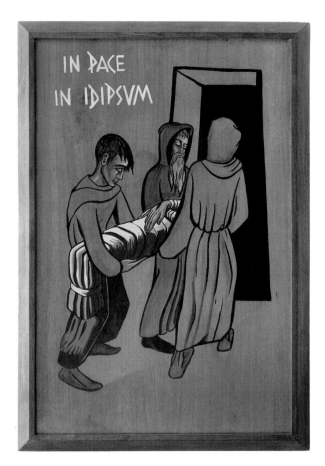

"In peace indeed."

HOLY DESIRE

FOURTEENTH STATION
Jesus Is Laid in the Tomb

In his *Rule* for monks, St. Benedict says that one must "keep death daily before your eyes" (*Rule* 4:47). And so here, the monastic artist provides a twist and pays tribute to his Benedictine heritage by portraying three monks carrying Christ's lifeless body into the tomb—which awaits us all.

This is not a macabre admonition or an invitation to be perpetually morose. Quite the opposite, as the preceding sentence in the passage from the *Rule* demonstrates: "Yearn for everlasting life with holy desire." Like the ancient Israelites, we are sojourners under the watchful and protecting gaze of our compassionate God as we travel to the Promised Land of eternal life through the love of Christ. The world as we know it is not the be-all and end-all. Something—or, more precisely, Someone—infinitely better awaits us. The joy of this knowledge, derived through faith, fills us with that holy desire needed to live radically here and now so that, as St. Benedict says toward the end of his *Rule*, Christ may bring us all together to everlasting life.

This is the hope that fills our days with joy without denying our deep sorrow. It is what makes us Christian. When things go terribly wrong, when failure and hardship seem to frame our days, and when people age and die, what we are really lamenting is the brokenness of Creation. We *should* feel sorrow, because the life for which God created us was not meant to be that way. However, we should *also* embrace the joy of knowing that in Christ, God has restored all things, and rightly ordered them as they are meant to be.

It is true that from our limited perspective, we cannot fully perceive that right-ordering. In Christ, however, the act has been completed, but is still growing to fulfillment. Similarly, when we plant a flower bulb in the earth during the lengthening shadows of autumn, we know that it will be months before it springs forth from the ground with life and color and fragrance— but its work has begun. The Incarnation continues to this very moment as the Body of Christ grows to maturity in each one of us. Truly, "with the Lord, one day is like a thousand years, and a thousand years are like one day" (2 Peter 3:8).

The moment has been redeemed, and eternity calls out to us from the dark moments just before the dawn. Listen, and from the silence of the tomb, cling to Jesus' words to his disciples the night before he died: "Do not let your hearts be troubled. Believe in God, believe also in me. In my Father's house there are many dwelling places. If I go and prepare a place for you, I will come again and will take you to myself, so that where I am, there you may be also. You know the way to the place where I am going…I am the way, and the truth, and the life" (John 14:1-4, 6).

PRAYER

Lord, I wait for the dawn of Resurrection
often in the midst of darkness and death.
Life is a struggle sometimes for all of us,
and we are overwhelmed by uncertainty
amid the passing days.
Our hearts long for eternity—for you.
However, by keeping death daily before our eyes,
we are encouraged to prepare rightly
for that moment when we will see your face.
Help us along the way—
in faith, hope, and love—to deny ourselves,
take up our cross daily and follow Christ,
forever trusting
that if we have been united with him in a death like his,
we will certainly be united with him
in a resurrection like his (cf. Luke 9:23; Romans 6:5).

If It Dies It Bears Much Fruit

~

To everyone who conquers,
I will give permission
to eat from the tree of life
that is in the paradise of God.

Revelation 2:7

~

A lifeless body in a tomb.

Alone.

Defeated.

Wrapped in burial cloths of misery, fear,
and failure.

A decaying grain concealed in darkest land.

Mystery awaits the morn.

Thin light spreads over a horizon unaware
of what the earth cannot contain.

The soil is soaked with divinity's dew.

The seed of humanity sheds its rotten garments.

The wound within opens.

A tender shoot appears.

It emerges above the soil.

Pulled toward the rising sun, it is green, full of sap.

Roots crack through and discard the seed's hard but fragile
casing…

… surge through and clutch the earth…

… drink from the brimming river.

The stalk grows thicker, taller.

Stems become branches.

Buds blossom and leaves unfurl.

Within them the birds of heaven sing their song.

Hanging there is ripened fruit.

Good for food.

Pleasing to the eye.

Desirable for gaining wisdom.

Fruit better than gold.

A woman enters the land.

She seeks a burial plot, and finds the tree.

She is amazed at what has arisen there.

Taking some of the fruit, she eats.

Urged by an angel, she shares it.

Naked again, eyes are opened.

Wrapped in the light of faith, hope, love.

Triumphant.

Together.

A vibrant body in a garden.

Planted in the house of the Lord.

Still bearing fruit when they are old.

Surrounding the Tree of Life.

Singing *Alleluia!*

About the Artist

Fr. Donald Walpole, O.S.B., (1917-2012), *was a Benedictine monk of Saint Meinrad Archabbey in Indiana. Born and raised in Indianapolis, he graduated from Saint Meinrad College in 1939, and professed vows as a monk in 1940. He was ordained to the priesthood in 1943. Receiving a Master of Fine Arts degree from the Art Institute of Chicago in 1952, he taught the history and practice of art to seminary undergraduates at Saint Meinrad for 45 years. His artworks are displayed not only throughout the monastery and seminary at Saint Meinrad, but also around the country. His glass mosaics, murals, window designs, and linen hangings are in cathedrals, parish churches, monasteries, convents, chapels, schools, mausoleums, and universities, from the Bahamas to Notre Dame to San Francisco.*

About the Author

Br. Francis de Sales Wagner, O.S.B., *is a Benedictine monk of Saint Meinrad Archabbey in Indiana, and is an editor and writer for Path of Life Publications at the Abbey Press. Born and raised in Findlay, Ohio, he received his undergraduate degree in journalism from Bowling Green State University in 1988. He worked as a staff writer, news editor, managing editor, copy editor, and wire editor for four daily newspapers in Ohio before coming to Saint Meinrad in 2006. He professed his vows as a monk in 2008, and in 2012 received a Master of Theological Studies degree in the School of Theology. He also serves as a conference presenter for the Benedictine oblate program and as a spiritual director. He is the author of several pastoral care publications and spirituality articles, and is editor of the book* Sacred Rhythms: The Monastic Way Every Day.